This Book Belongs To

. . . .

WELCOME TO COUNT THE LAWN MOWERS

Count all the lawn mowers like this one!

Congratulations! You guessed.
There are three such lawn mowers:

Count all the lawn mowers like this one!

Congratulations! You guessed.
There are two such lawn mowers:

2

Count all the lawn mowers like this one!

Congratulations! You guessed.
There are three such lawn mowers :

3

Count all the lawn mowers like this one!

Congratulations! You guessed.
There is one such lawn mower:

1

Count all the lawn mowers like this one!

Congratulations! You guessed.
There are two such lawn mowers:

2

Count all the lawn mowers like this one!

Congratulations! You guessed.
There are four such lawn mowers:

Count all the lawn mowers like this one!

Congratulations! You guessed.
There are two such lawn mowers:

2

Count all the lawn mowers like this one!

Congratulations! You guessed.
There are two such lawn mowers:

2

How many orange lawn mowers are here?

Congratulations! You guessed.
There is one such lawn mower in orange color:

1

How many white lawn mowers are here?

Congratulations! You guessed.
There are two such lawn mowers in white color:

2

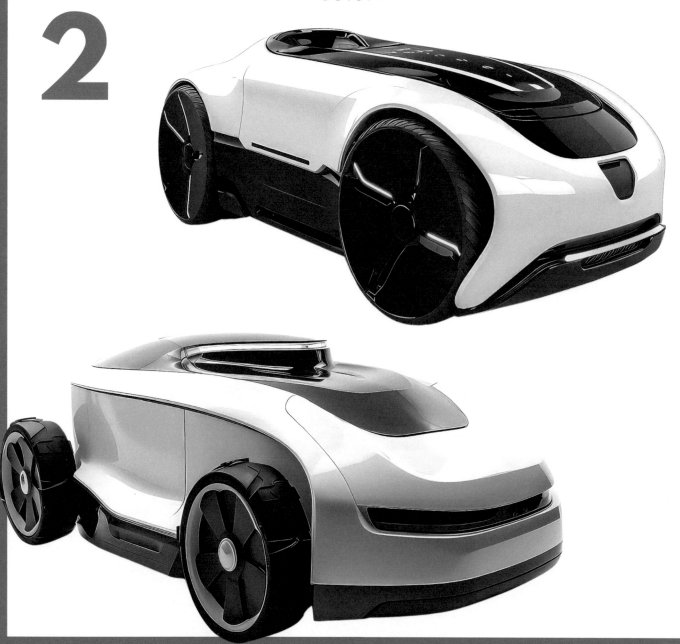

How many green lawn mowers are here?

Congratulations! You guessed.
There are three such lawn mowers in green color:

3

How many red lawn mowers are here?

Congratulations! You guessed.
There are two such lawn mowers in red color:

Find two of the same lawn mowers:

Congratulations! You guessed.
There are two of the same lawn mowers:

How many lawn mowers are here?

Congratulations! You guessed.
There are five lawn mowers:

1

2

3

4

5

How many lawn mowers are here?

Congratulations! You guessed.
There are six lawn mowers:

Made in United States
Troutdale, OR
12/27/2024